# A CRY IN THE SNOW

THE FRENCH LIST

# A CRY IN THE SNOW

## AND OTHER POEMS

Stella Vinitchi Radulescu

TRANSLATED BY LUKE HANKINS

LONDON NEW YORK CALCUTTA

Grateful acknowledgment is made to the editors of the following periodicals, where some of these translations originally appeared: *Advaitam Speaks Literary, Asheville Poetry Review, Blue Lyra Review, The Chattahoochee Review, Connotation Press: An Online Artifact, Levure littéraire, Obra/Artifact, Pleiades, New Poetry in Translation, Verse* (online), *Waxwing* and *World Literature Today*. A selection of these translations was also published as a limited edition chapbook, *I Was Afraid of Vowels . . . Their Paleness*, by Q Avenue Press (USA) in 2011.

Thanks to Patrice Kanoszai of Éditions du Cygne and Paul Van Melle of Éditions du Gril for granting translation rights.

**Seagull Books, 2018**

This collection includes translations from two volumes:

*Un cri dans la neige* by Stella Vinitchi Radulescu
© Éditions du Cygne (Paris), 2009

*Journal aux yeux fermés* by Stella Vinitchi Radulescu
© Éditions du Gril (Belgium), 2010

English translation © Luke Hankins, 2018

ISBN   978 0 8574 2 597 3

**British Library Cataloguing-in-Publication Data**
A catalogue record for this book is available from the British Library.

Typeset by Seagull Books, Calcutta, India
Printed and bound by Maple Press, York, Pennsylvania, USA

# CONTENTS

*Translator's Note* | *vii*

I. *A Cry in the Snow* | 1

first mornings | 3

sphere | 4

landscape in three movements | 5

adagio | 6

ghost of a day | 7

definition | 8

children of the fog | 9

the earth begins | 10

the earth begins (2) | 11

just as I fall silent | 12

body to body | 13

alone under the shifting vault | 14

interior | 15

here where the body | 16

what you think | 17

memory keep still | 18

sometimes in the evening | 19

that is to say | 20

exotics | 21

day and night | 23

there will be voices | 24

the day's fatigue | 26

autumn confession | 28

if time owns me | 29

others | 30

evidence | 31

a cry in the snow | 32

*The Public Rose* | 33

if I remember it's in order to forget again | 35

after you november evening | 36

house on fire | 37

a cry in the snow (2) | 39

the clock however | 40

from door to door | 41

there where I am | 42

the dialogue is growing thin | 43

posthumous inventory | 44

that's the calendar | 46

what life on earth is about | 47

morning   I'm leaving | 48

II. *Journal with Closed Eyes* | 49

III. *Fragments of Life and Death* | 79

I believe Stella Vinitchi Radulescu to be one of the most under-appreciated living poets in any language. Her work provides a crucial historical and aesthetic link to communist-era Eastern Europe, while also being deeply influenced by French surrealism and American modernism. And she is in rare company indeed as a poet who writes in three languages.

Radulescu was born in Romania and began writing poetry at an early age. She eventually published several collections in Romania. 'Writing poetry was risky,' Radulescu says, 'it could have been seen as "a political manifesto" against the regime!—but it was also a refuge.'

In 1983, at the height of Ceaușescu's communist regime, Radulescu left Romania. After seeking political asylum in Rome, she immigrated to the US and began writing poetry in English, discovering novel dimensions of expression through writing in a third language. She attributes part of her success in this area to her study of linguistics. She also continued to write in French, which was always 'la langue de la poésie' for her. She points to the fact that Samuel Beckett wanted to write deliberately in French, and asserts that 'there is always something mysterious about the language.'

Radulescu does not translate any of her own poems, and thus has a distinct body of work in each of her three languages. As she puts it: 'I feel, think, act, perceive, smell, touch differently according to the language I write in.' Radulescu's latest book of original

English-language poetry is *I Scrape the Window of Nothingness: New & Selected Poems* (Orison Books, 2015). She has been kind enough to allow me to translate her French poetry, and I gratefully acknowledge her partnership in finalizing the translations that appear here.

*Luke Hankins*

I

## A CRY IN THE SNOW

. . . *space of a cry*
        *surrounded by*
*space*
        *surrounded by*
            *nothing.*

Lorand Gaspar

# first mornings

at the break of dawn
juncture of the seasons    the earth warms

the text is read on one's knees

the sea kneeling between stones

the world's first mornings smooth mornings
mornings of war

cold and heat        we will enter our houses
of flesh
hands spread like vast horizons

we will taste what is written
on these lips        the foam of a wave the nonchalance
of gestures—

as I advance and step into daylight
I see forms expanding
in the mirror of the hours

: the men who set out at sunrise to meet
their lives

## sphere

here we are
the earth in our bowels

the sphere
the taste of happiness

the tortoise aligns itself with the voice
the period

with the comma approach
furtively

but about what
about what

do the stars speak to us

# landscape in three movements

sand becomes water
wind, desire

: undulation reaching the borders of the soul

the incestuous night opens at the Word
like a woman's body

here is the sea that struts with small distant
steps

a wave draws near
and asks itself

where to break the silence

# adagio

a sound rises    a whiteness
from the region of the heart

autumn of slow breath    stiff
bones of light

the fires in the garden have died down
: cities of the past

sleeping cities
I was afraid of vowels    their paleness

beneath the moon
the nighthorses moving away

at a trot
no

it's not a word not yet    this vapour
escaping the mouth

## ghost of a day

come forward, then       black night's feet
silver mouth

      a statue also dies
      ghost of a day
      work of a sleeping god

your furtive lover's gesture
caught in the web of the gaze     the spider

      and its cross

      celestial linens on the unmade bed
: light

that appears rumpled

## definition

that it were yesterday          or:

choose between the faces
chiselled in marble on the dunes of air

the verbs without memory

the memory of the stars
conjugate the insomnia of coming nights

the light which prostitutes itself on the street-corner
forgetfulness on the page :

desperately night

story of us

history in ashes

# children of the fog

children of the fog
dense fog of those eyes      gazes
intersecting
the paths of meteors

sons and daughters of the forbidden blue
years stained
black with forgetfulness

the dearest of my sisters      life
at the entrance to the garden
where grow blooming bodies and beatific moons

rose    rosemary

## the earth begins

the earth begins one distant afternoon
with the breast's
ochre colour
the transparent milk that flows and the mouth
that takes pleasure in it

with the memory of another land
which has just left us

the fear of losing it          the breast withdrawn
the milk dried up

look—the earth is beginning
today
and ends with me as I wait     you'd call it
a withered place

pinched between two fingers of silence

## the earth begins (2)


the earth begins on the smooth page     taut belly
exposed to the knife

an incision makes the red flow     I touch the words
roll them    hide them in my pockets

I erase their borders
I invent sleepful mornings

towards which dreams set out with slow steps like camels
and disappear

far away in the desert of the hours

**just as I fall silent**


just as I fall silent beneath the branches
your voice dresses in gold and green

dances
displaces the air
destroys time

                    what separates us :
the blue within the reach of the mouth

I leave my clothes at the feet of this unknown god—

are you familiar with him?

## body to body

the tree in place of my thirst

I plant it in my eyes

I send its roots
into my veins

I stretch myself in the black     I watch
its sparkling

stars     I whisper my secrets
into its leaves
I wake with a start

I smile

I fly     I grow green

I fade into the shadow of the tree

## alone under the shifting vault


and the mauve of a passing thought        am I
this body struggling with itself
next to me

the world at hand        the twitch of a mouth
about to speak
as one speaks in the fallen evening
with the angels

: I've grown quiet        don't want to sleep
at the price of a day and the one who carries
the lamp
his steps this violence in the throat the yes the no

I cover myself in sounds
and I walk

## interior

I wake in my own body and then
in the other
waking beside me
jealous that I stirred first

wall of sounds :

barricade the night
crack language in half     the earth clutches
the void
what's left of it . . .

I stretch out on the beach
no wave carries me away     as the day
we're still talking about
approaches . . .

## here where the body

here where the body hollowed out its bed
and its hands

voracious plants still grow          this transparence
turning purple

unspoken languages cling
like vines
to the body

the eyelids rise    the eyes learn
to open

colours and shapes          green and red fish
swim past

through a patch of light
in the murky depths of night                    white pebbles

these minutes

I'm here I stand up          I signal you
my body in the current

you name it          it drifts aimlessly

## what you think

*like a good god I reconsider*
*and send you the message of the rain*

God says and casually closes his eyes

blood flows I get up open the curtains the jasmine
remains silent
the blue trembles

I'm thirsty
I light the candles

the dry season begins once again

## memory keep still

at the bottom of the glass            *memory keep still*

the drop sits like that

whether

a river

whether a tear      a solemn day

comes

a day of white tenderness

the world returns to it


I'll no longer finish

being born

## sometimes in the evening

no it's not me here          for quite some time
someone has enjoyed inhabiting my days
and my nights

lacking myself I practice innocence I make love
with the shadows
when they lie down on the sidewalk

and I fill out the absence forms
with my blood
sometimes in the evening I hear a voice and its echo saying

*the rain the rain and the blooming lilacs*
*childhood* :

this snail that hides itself in the shell of my life

**that is to say**


the grief of the day on the church tower

the dog that barks in the streets of sleep

our images come out of their boxes and sit on the stones

the frontiers expand between words and sounds
that is to say here we are

drifting and in the troughs of the breakers we hear sirens

and the dead who say hello to us
in an ancient language

## exotics

your exotic bird mouth says hello     I swallow
sound
after sound

I caress the vowels

who wants to see me as a little stream flowing out of
    the dark
leaping over the grass

watering the flowerbeds of absence?

~

touch the flesh     the wind knows nothing about it

walk on the tip of these words     a fire starts

the world trembles

bitter pleasure decked out in sequins and feathers

a man glides in my sleep opens my chest

with an axe

~

we see the sky and the stars          the night wobbles

on my lips

I climb time I defend myself

with a pale

smile

## day and night

day and night happiness rummages
through the garbage
like a homeless old woman

down to the depths of souls the war
of the roses
the withered roses *ah! the unwritten*
*poem waits for me*

on the sidewalk:     people have
already wiped everything clean
with their smiles of hatred

## there will be voices

perhaps there will be eyes that by some miracle
escape the view of the streets
of cadavers

: the white storm of the century
forests
of reaching hands

anonymity
of a human mouth

~

perhaps there will be mouths that by some miracle
escape words

deserted

: the desert with its stars up for auction to the highest
    bidder

~

to name
the stolen happiness

the bird the child the flowering meadow :

perhaps there will be voices

an echo repeating

## the day's fatigue

this wound

on the surface of the earth

I climb the hill

the sunset meets me

I hide in my heart

one beat more

I beg you

early or late

there will be plenty left

to die from

this fluorescent love

as if plunged

into night

we could

one within the other

give new birth

to the coming dawn

## autumn confession

*I will have said everything, and no one in this corner
to distinguish my hands from my face.*

Joë Bousquet

the song is in the pause    the trough
of the wave

lace of sounds        the view    someone is talking to me
loudly

: autumn has never seemed so bright and sweet
listen

the bells      the distant echo

the nowhere

of my days

## if time owns me

it's because I'm still wearing
his old clothes

and his worn-out shoes and I let myself get swept away
by his old-fashioned ways and I don't want

to go back a single moment nor cry on a rock
and expose myself naked

tearing off the veil of light

**others**


two hours into time's memory and the clockhand
stops like a dead man's heart

and yet this cry

the silhouettes of the hours

where are you coming from song?

who is signalling me?

others live on Earth        someone far away
can see us moving forward

rubber boots

gazes lost in the snow

## evidence

the evidence is killing me   how can I escape it
let myself be devoured by the night
its blue colours its stealthy footsteps
its dishonest ways

how much can I hate the view
the eye taking pleasure in the deceptive distance

theatre of the day :
are we more alive or more dead
little toys

in time's pocket?

**a cry in the snow**


at the brim of night
a fire leaps up an arm gestures to me

my presence
seems to make the roses tremble
in the garden

and make the birds rise up
and make the earth shake

the streets lengthen       the shadow of an infinite
word
haunts the minutes haunts

the hours
I want to remain silent but my cry attaches itself
to a sliver of light

the snow covers it
with its suffocating coolness       a loving gesture
before the cold

in the burning mouth

## The Public Rose

*I've long had a useless face . . .*

Paul Éluard

neglected flowers       the garden

weeps

in blue       chew up this angel

: it will snow slowly

a childhood

on the streets

~

a skeleton here

the self

this red

standing in the tree of the evening       as if already

someone on earth were watching

my return

## if I remember it's in order to forget again

: hands drenched in night sweat
we hesitated
before every door

colliding with myself I learned fear
our steps grew long

like snakes        if I remember
it's in order to forget again

the last gesture I had to make        the doorway the house
I never entered

you hid behind words waiting far away for my voice
and then the dream

the dream I never dreamed        oceanic depths
on sealed lips

when words were still in use

## after you november evening

two words are all I need to speak you to pronounce you

to carry you on the silent backs of camels

to cross the desert

but the third races up to us at the crossroads

and flips onto its side

~

after you

november evening
cold falls on the lips like an unknown language

the withered bay-tree of waiting at night's doorway

I'm entering the era of the flood   a wave erases the word
*tomorrow*

## house on fire

the tiles are made of silver
the birds of clay

the smoking house twists
coils up into the trees seeking

the spark
that once set it

on fire

~

: drops drops and who is it and what is it
at the doors
and windows who or what is groping
infinity

my shadow at the corner of the street is doing laundry
cleaning the dishes

and washing away the day's blood

~

sleep boasts about me

I escape it      cling to the voice      she's the rose

and I'm the thorn

life sprouting next to us

## a cry in the snow (2)

I shout my sovereign cry
smashing the silence

: there is still a cadaver to identify
: there is still a life to live and then from which
    direction will the snow
begin its white its long funerals

I walk forward without memory I have a new body
I love its nakedness     imagine the vase    time
in alabaster

which without any light dazzles your eyes

## the clock however

the clock however doesn't get used to the rain
it wobbles
and the train stops at another station

oh the things invented by the rain!

drops of happiness      which flow and dance
that's what we would need tonight
to cross over death

## from door to door

crossing the country

from stone to stone

under the vault of the evening

up to my neck in falling leaves

words keeping watch on me

so much silence in my bones I forget

my name

my parents left me

with nowhere to go

so many tears

so many whispers

on the next page

## there where I am

there where I am          where fear          where words

their hungry mouths

*you're violating the poem abusing it*
*so much charm and so much forgetting*

*stop I'm bleeding*

and the sound like a distant boat

you repeat me infinitely

## the dialogue is growing thin


the afternoon rummages
through the dresser and underneath
the sea

where once I kept my eyes open
like two large bubbles

of air

back when I named things and put them
in their proper places

before shutting my eyelids

## posthumous inventory

**1.**

a man suspended from a rose his throat
burns
the key forgotten under the door

                                      the rain
and the afternoon

three petals and the words for them
the habit of singing one's life
that which polishes itself that which goes without saying
bends, articulates

the uncertainty of being here among so many things
that must be named

: the evening like a buffalo
: the sea like a breath
: your face like a candle
a street to the right the other in the sky    alas

applaud
love which hides itself in the train stations
the pale colours
the lovers in bloom       daffodils   cherry trees

the great deserts

the chiaroscuro


2.

consciousness awakening          the pillow sinks
in a dreamlake

the mundane puts on its straw hat:

a beautiful day spent in the company of others


3.

the snow will melt I will be silent
you will cheep in your tombs the verbs
will roll freely on the page someone
will speak like a god something
will be called a city
or sand
we will seek shelter in a conch

so light so light

almost imperceptible . . .

## that's the calendar


without months

without days or seasons

sand and sky

the wound

get used

to the noise of the hours  the flesh

that jumps underneath the flesh


: who can untangle our lips

from blueness

# what life on earth is about

in the garden among the leaves

have the birds gone away?

where is this noise at the bottom of the ocean coming from

this avalanche of human forms?


enough? of course not, it's starting again

the empire is drowning

they're hanging innocents

and it's up to the wind to listen to their cries

to soften their souls

**morning      I'm leaving**


to meet the sun
hat of air shoes of fresh dirt

the hours follow me          day approaches
intoxicated by my footsteps :

so little of you
between two strikes of the bell


~


I keep going       a little path opens up
through the tangle          the body

pale purple
: the colour of twilight

and I stop at the crossroads to bury
a tear

at the foot of the sycamore

II

## JOURNAL WITH CLOSED EYES

*Every flower grows in a prison.*

Salvador Dalí

The August heat pierces me to the core. The flies too. And his patched-up pyjamas. He had to sell his gold watch to some neighbours . . . Soon, very soon, his life will be over. Sitting on the edge of the bed, his breathing shallow . . . He asks me for a cigarette.

First I stand up, then I find the pack, next . . . But is there really an order to things? I've made and repeated these motions for such a long time, always the same, backwards and forwards, I extend my hand, I find the pack, I light the cigarette, I know it won't burn to the end.

The sun through the windows is already making me sweat. The next room over, the children are waking up. The lapping of their little voices.

You could begin a book this way. Or end one.

7 November. They assemble us in The Square.

The Square, decorated in red, flags and portraits. My friend next to me in her marine blue coat and little wool cap. She's shaking from the cold, she's shaking for fear, she's shaking out of love for her mother she can't see anymore.

A truck has arrived during the night. In silence. The silence of footsteps that don't return. *Siberia—is that far? No, not as far as death.* But the day doesn't want to end, nor the cold. Her mouth opens at regular intervals like a valve, chants: *sta – lin, sta – lin.*

The voice multiplies, resounds through the crowd. The crowd in the mirror, double-sided mirror. Agony of the seasons. She takes my hand and looks at me. Her mouth open, her eyes remain mute.

*And can you describe* that? a woman asks Akhmatova in the line in front of the prisons of Leningrad.

*Yes, I can,* she responds.

The executioner washes his hands after the ceremony. The spring water is a transparent pink, the blood has lost its colour. The wind has fallen silent.

Black uniforms, black angels, we are leaving the earth. Who has seen us, who has known us?

She looks at me, the faceless woman, I can sense it, but I can't see her eyes. My heart is beating hard. She's moving away. I want to get closer to her, or at least for her to speak to me. I hear unknown words, what language is this . . . Even this, these sounds, I can only catch between long pauses.

I realize that I'm the one moving away, I'm taking steps, huge steps in the other direction. She wants to approach and touch my face. I'm watching her from a distance. I have no face. Her heart is beating hard . . .

Winter,

I have to wake up.
The day enters the room. With the leavings of yesterday. The first things that reach my ears, fragments of conversation, unfinished phrases. I lie down again. I forget the beginnings of sentences . . .

Invent the walls, one by one, the window in front of you, the door to the left. Across the darkness.

Find yourself back in your body, fall . . . There is no other way.

I cover myself in words.

If I don't describe things precisely, no one will read them.

The dogs barked the whole night. This is my distant childhood. We had to cross a river, someone took me in their arms. The yellow lampshade in the corner of the room and the barking dogs. When they stop barking I hear echoes. I stuff my head into the pillow, but I still hear them. The deserted streets of sleep.

Tonight my father gets up, totters around in his tomb, raises a sickly arm and closes the window.

Now it's past midnight, you're far away. The whales and the animals at the bottom of the ocean sleep while our thoughts roam the surface.

Yesterday I bought the poems of Vallejo, in English. He surprises and disturbs me every time I open the book. So I close it, I put it aside. But there are verses that haunt me, *this evening it's raining more than ever; and I have no desire to live, heart . . .*

It's raining in Romania. I've just come back from school, I'm running, soaked, especially my shoes. What will I wear tomorrow? I make it home. The evening speeds by. Mama isn't back yet. I hear children shouting outside, the screeching of a tramway . . . I open the blue notebook.

The pages have scattered on the beach. Letters fall off, wrap around rocks, fray, twist, attach to the roots of plants, strange organisms, writhing seaweed . . .

A melody rises from the earth. Suddenly I recognize it, it's the one I put on in the car sometimes. Then it changes. I hear footsteps underground . . .

Untangle these letters, gather them from the sand, it's my job, I'm the one who has to do it, I know it.

I'm the one who invented them, drew them with coloured pencils in my notebook.

And I can't move, my feet, my steps . . .

This seaweed that grows out of me . . .

In black there is every colour. The orange of our love, the pearl grey of waiting, interwoven hands the colour of forgetting, the pink dust of thought covering the furniture, the uncoloured profile of a man searching for the exit and asking me over and over what time it is and which train he needs to take and what country . . .

Of which you spoke to me.

Of which you speak to me and the silence of your words presses into me like a new plant the colour of this life.

I've been doing laundry all night. The blood won't come out of the sheets. I'm going to the drugstore tomorrow to get some bleach. You can put it in the water, they say you can do that, then dry the sheets in the sun. I remember a wrinkled hand folding and cleaning . . .

A dreamlike gesture, as if it were forgotten for a second in mid-air, a hand smoothing the surface of this world, smooth and clean, translucent.

My bed isn't made. If someone knocks on the door, I won't open it anymore.

**Bloodred.**

*Amethyst . . . the color that corresponds to the change of an era in the world.*

Dalí

I recognize the prison by the reflections of sunlight and the odour of mould. And sometimes, I see it.

The sun draws bars in the air through which birds enter and exit. Invisible.
But I sense them. They fall.
They spin.
They die. I hold them for a second at eye level, where, in the gaps between the light, they can still retain their form.

And I hear cries, human cries, when the wind blows from the east. Therefore, I can distinguish my own cry. I bend over, discover my body in the grass.

It's Friday and the crucifixion has not yet taken place. So I'm told.

There were jonquils, and then there was a great sadness.
In people's eyes.

The trains always stopped too far from our house and
departed too early. We'd walk to the station and some-
times a bit of happiness would make us run and cross
the tracks without looking around and so we had
already arrived just like that and we saw the field of jon-
quils on our right, having had no idea that beauty even
existed or that it could exist in any form whatsoever . . .
We sat on the new grass and, eyes half-closed as if to
better retain the sight of the field, we ate what we had
put in our backpack the evening before, bread and
cheese.

As soon as I bought a notebook I was sure that I'd fill it. The first page was already the last.

Time hurries me onward. It speeds up. There are still a few minutes and I have to get to the station, cross the streets and the waiting room, the sleeping bodies with open mouths, the dirty benches and the breathing full of weariness and alcohol. It's written in my destiny that I must pass this place, and the hours, without respite, without reason, shuffle past.

Remember, a certain month of that year,

a certain day of that month, on the quay ... If I had at least left ...

With a scalpel just the right size for each, thoughts are extracted. Torture without pain and leaving no trace. We content ourselves with little, very little indeed. We're grateful for what we don't have. We spy on one another in the halls and are ashamed of ourselves.

—*Hate each other!*
—*Okay!*

Walls are growing from the ground. Someone is whispering in the small rooms, little coffee cups, little alleyways, little world cut from the larger script, little trembling hands, little portions of life.

Suddenly you find that you've grown too old.

I invent a style to fit this long day. I won't respond to you anymore, I need time to better situate myself in the late light of this day and to gather clothes for the winter.

It's already snowing in Bucharest. I buy a grey wool sweater and hurry back.

No one clears the snow. The streets are packed with it, you can hardly get anywhere. No one goes out. Puddles form in the intersections, but no one cares.

Snow—the only whiteness of that time.

You can rearrange these pages. There is no order, no sequence. You can erase lines, add others, switch out the events.

It's up to you. I won't respond anymore. Too busy staying silent. I would have liked to have spoken to you about my life but I don't feel up to it. I only say what I want you to know, and you don't want even that.

For some time everything's been out of place, and things have never gone back where they belong.

I won't respond to you anymore because I've forgotten the taste of snow. Each winter it snows less and less.

I continue. Thursday.

I can no longer escape this book. Voracious. It's as if it were already written and doesn't want me to expose it to the light, to send it into the world. I wake during the night and it threatens me, clings to me—I'm sick of it.

And you who think I write in the comfort of my room, in the warmth of a sunny day, in the luxury of your declarations of love . . .

Thursday. The same. Seven days and time hasn't budged. I've escaped it. Seven times seven units of time that no longer have a name. They're burying mother. I'm the one who carries her up the hill in a bag that's very heavy. The more I climb, the heavier it gets. I stumble, I have to make it, the bells are ringing . . . I'm still far away . . .

I'm reading a novel on a bench near the lake. The beach is empty, soon summer will arrive with all the noise and all the colours.

Two children in the distance, their ball rising into the air: a small incision in the blue.

This ball. The arc it makes in the air. It falls on the other side of time, in our old garden, in the country we've abandoned. I catch it in flight and night descends so gently I see souls dressed in white coming to meet it.

And I see myself, sitting there, listening to the descent of night on the hills. The blooming cherry trees of a palpable beauty . . .

*. . . such an abyss I'm lost in. Especially in the morning as the day begins. To find my voice, the tone . . . so many things that need to be said, which have been waiting for an eternity to be said, waiting since yesterday.*

I read late into the night and my father notices the light. The room is cold, we don't have enough wood to heat it. The door creaks a little and I see him . . . *scraps of time, sparks beneath the ashes, memory crumbles . . .*

I see him enter, his long-fingered hand on my forehead, *Sleep, now* . . . I've never known such tenderness.

The nights are very long and the days pass unnoticed. I hear thoughts like little motors whirring in the air. Others' thoughts and my own. Living, keeping me company, more alive than those to whom they belong.

Over the years some have grown hard with rust; others, weakening, falling apart, still delight me. So I wind them up, set the little motors going, and I listen to them . . .

I'd have a hard time waking tomorrow to find only silence.

It's three in the morning, the dead in their graves. I think of them. Thought is alive, warm, it gathers itself, forms a kernel that attaches itself to the world, and it begins to move, to shift.

I give the dead this gift, the only one possible.

The dead—a formless mass on which we walk.

Today and always.

Autumn. Eternal like a long love poem for someone who can't read it. Because he's the one who is writing it from afar, without words, with the breeze and these strident colours that nauseate me. He who stripped himself of hours and seasons in order to become this long stretch of time, this endless poem.

Futile to set the clock. Existence measured by little events, and then everything collapses into an infinite word.

We took long walks and collected dry leaves, and we spoke softly in the pale light of the streetlamps on a bench that no longer exists. In a town that lights up, goes dark, and lights up once again, like a distant boat in the fog.

I'm going to the mountain. I watch the white crests. I see the sun. I'm climbing. The sun follows me. I can't open my eyes anymore. I'm wearing an ugly dress and worn-out shoes. I'm listening to music. I'm climbing. I'm sweating. I'm listening to music. I brush my hair. I buy a mirror. I'm so young!

No, you can never imagine such youth. Happiness is hiding in the folds of my dress, which I touch with a nervous hand. The sensation of tearing the light; my body is one of the shreds . . .

Who knows me in this blue desert of thought? I'm walking and without knowing it I give happiness a name, and the trees take up the echo.

I said, this victory, today, is made of my losses, of all my failures, built on my days of waiting, on my empty nights.

I said, this glory . . . The paragraphs I never finished— you stole their letters from me. Even if you gave them back today, it would be too late; the spaces have been filled.

They were gesticulating and holding their hands out to me with books to sign. I said, these are the hours I haven't lived, the circles that never closed because you cut holes in my eyes.

There were lots of people, men and women, come for the celebration. An immense moon rose out of the lake. Sickening red.

Someone next to me put on a Piaf album; she sang *Padam, Padam* . . .

Sign what? I said.

They crowded around me and held out a book I didn't recognize.

I don't cry. I look at the poster I bought at the museum in Philadelphia: Brancusi, "The Kiss." Across from the bed, hung on the wall. It reminds me of Magritte's "The Rape": the violence of flesh.

Empty boxes in my head, this heart that wrestles too much with itself. The way one goes on in this world. Whatever happens.

I close the computer.

I'm glad I never knew you and that you continue to exist in the part of the world where the windows open on flowering fields and one watches the sheep, where people say, like you, *This is where happiness begins.*

I live in an unknown village. You can smell salt and sea-weed here, but you can't see the sea. The more I look for it, the more elusive it becomes. A warm breeze blows and the men, in shirtsleeves, build dams. Some days pass more quickly than others, and there are few women. You can't tell the colour of their eyes. I want to plant trees—I bought a shovel—but they won't let me do it. There are strict rules and streets with no address. Dogs eat one another. I seem to catch glimpses of some-one signalling me with a motion of their hand.

To get here, I often take the six o'clock train. I rarely return.

III

# FRAGMENTS OF LIFE AND DEATH

I lived in the time of lilacs and empty eyes. Find a fulcrum,
a horizon.

A straight line,
a fixed point.

Changeful history carried us with it like a tide ...     A
    sudden revelation:

night and all it drags along, letters, uncompleted
    sentences,
do you remember the sand?

We were happy to live and wait for the moon to dissipate
    the clouds,

but you others,
who measure happiness with your tears—*that's the way
    it is,*

*paradise lost,*

says the poet.

To write is to forgive. My poems are so proud of
    forgiving silences for their silence,

the sky for hiding behind thick clouds: a lonely blue,
    absent words,

what doesn't last,

our lives,

shipwrecks . . .

Our house was in the sky, perched on a hill of clouds,
    a branch of the apple tree crossed the courtyard,
    stones yellowed by the years that had passed since
    my birth.


The house was small. It seemed large to me. Few
    windows.

On each wall I drew rectangles, and the light came in,
    pink at first,
then violet, and finally black, I so wanted to rid myself
    of my past.

Then a tear fell, and it was more human . . .


*Tremble*, I said to the leaves of the apple tree, and they
    began to tremble. I loved that movement of air
    that refreshed my memory.

What, then?

Everything crashed to the ground with a deafening
    noise, except the music of the withered leaves, the
    chattering rain, the silence that crackled in the
    corners like the fire in the chimney,

the insurmountable nights of our former lives.

The courtyard is square, the apple tree blossoming.
    My mother

is cooking, my father should be on his way home,
    my sentences are starting
to connect.

*Hold fast, my children,* I heard his voice, night was falling
with no reason, people were very afraid.

Fear solidifies, takes the shape of a branch, or rather the
    night,
or a ferocious animal lurking in the corner.

Fear is dreadful, the war showing in my parents' eyes . . .

At the end of folly, remorse:

what you haven't done, what you could have done, thick
    walls,
they've turned the old chateaus in the east into prisons,
    no sound

crosses the borders: the weight of stone.

By contrast, inside, flute music rises from the floor,
prisoners dressed in stripes
lean to hear it . . .

The battlefield was close to us and really everywhere,
there were people who died where they stood

as if
some solar event had struck the living.

I gathered what they left, their last words, and arranged
     them
in the poem,

oh yes, I could more or less see the line of demarcation,
     *The gods are*

*in the metaphor*, said René Char.

*The Empty Rooms*, the title of my last collection.
    Metaphors
work well,

empty of what?
What can you put in a room?

Everything and nothing.

Lying under the stars, fill the void that grows in you,
furnish your solitude,

attach the hours one to the next, it's quick work:

a life.

I'm writing a book on my future life, which I imagine
    comparable to my current one. I'll still eat wild
    grass,

spell words from an ancient dictionary out loud—all
    things told, I'll be just as I am. The moon hides
    and my eyes open,

immense.

What luck to be on earth . . .

I saw blooming cherry trees climbing the gentle

slope

towards a sacred place whose name I've forgotten
where perhaps the world found its reason for existing—

dreams faded
martyrs of a thirsty world, a world hungry for a forbidden
    blankness,

condemned to bury the bodies and create new ones

witness or accused
I'm still alive

memories have no age.

I was approaching with slow steps, pretending
to be looking for something in the grass,

stretching the distances . . .

I arrive. Description of the prison: suddenly
night's tomb. Silence becomes impenetrable,

the walls transparent, you can see
the hearts beating inside, as if on a rope

that shines in the dark, and the swirling
thoughts with no way
out      yes,

the thoughts are part of a visible universe,

a palpable universe,
it was there

the prison        women men together

*Draw me a sheep* and hundreds of stars
will shine:

we'll no longer be of this world,
which we'll carry
on our great migratory birds' wings

beyond what the eye can see          the clamour
of new lands

can you hear it?

I'd like to tell stories that never happened, otherwise . . .

A wall. I jump over it.

Look!
I don't want to look. The flowering narcissus embalms
    the air.

Graves and more graves.
Who? Us?

Look!
I don't want to look. All the deaths are the same. There
    will be no celebration, these are the
    anonymous.

We're the anonymous.

And the last thing I wanted to imagine, a river that
    flows at our feet and carries us far away . . .

Pell-mell, we gather the dead.

The living we kill.

We take the birds embroidered on blouses to mass.

We light candles to signal our victory, the high tide of
    evening rising:

the beach is glutted with people.

The erotic heat of a voracious plant clings to the
heart,

final words engulfed by the current,
we don't finish our sentences,

sweet absences,

the trembling white of vowels

and everything one can't think any more        adrift

there are still mouths

starving
and bodies that want to be touched

and bodies that want to be stars . . .